Cut Your TAX in 2010

And Preserve Your Legacy

by Anthony R. Perrelli and Dean R. Hedeker
with LuAnn Glowacz

NEW YEAR PUBLISHING LLC
DANVILLE, CALIFORNIA

Cut Your Tax in 2010 and Preserve Your Legacy
by Anthony R. Perrelli and Dean R. Hedeker with LuAnn Glowacz

First Edition
COPYRIGHT © 2010 HEDEKER & PERRELLI, LTD.

Copyright © 2010 by New Year Publishing, LLC
144 Diablo Ranch Court
Danville, CA 94506 USA
http://www.newyearpublishing.com

ISBN 978-1-9355470-5-1
Library of Congress Control Number: 2009941704

All rights reserved. No part of this book may be reproduced or transmitted in any form or by any means, electronic or mechanical, including photocopying, recording or by any information storage and retrieval system, without written permission from the publisher, except for the inclusion of brief quotations in a review.

*To our families and clients,
who inspire us every day*

Please Note

This book is a general overview of basic legal concepts. The tax, legal, and investment issues mentioned in this book vary considerably from jurisdiction to jurisdiction, and they may change at any time. Please consult a lawyer or tax adviser in your area who is knowledgeable about your state's current laws if you have a specific legal or tax question. This information is not intended to be a substitute for specific individualized tax, legal, or investment planning advice.

Although New Year Publishing and the authors have used best efforts in providing practical, useful information in this book, they make no representations or warranties as to its accuracy or completeness. Additionally, they do not make any implied warranties of merchantability or fitness for a particular purpose.

Advice given in this book is not guaranteed or warranted, and it may not be suitable advice for every situation. Neither New Year Publishing nor the authors shall be liable for any losses suffered by any reader of this book. Content that addresses investment strategies specifically is solely advice from co-author Dean Hedeker, a Registered Financial Consultant.

We strongly insist that you discuss your specific tax, legal, and investment strategies with a qualified lawyer or tax adviser.

All scenarios given in this book are fictional unless otherwise noted, and any resemblance to actual persons or events is coincidental.

Contents

Author Accolades viii
Acknowledgements ix
Introduction x

1. Reasons to Rethink What You're Doing 1
   Uncle Sam needs your money now 3
   Tax advantages in 2010. 6
   Every plan needs maintenance 8

2. You're Richer Than You Think 11
   Why Uncle Sam thinks you're rich 13
   Change the way you view your money 15

3. Capital Gains Trap 19
   Capital gains in a nutshell 22
   Back to the Richards 26
   What you should do 31

4. Protect Your Assets in 4 Steps 33

5. Step 1: Convert to Roth IRAs. 37
   The beauty of recharacterization 40
   2010: Year of the Roth IRA. 41
   Meet Sally Smith, semi-retiree. 42
   Lost your job? Get a Roth IRA 45

6. Step 2: Invest to Reduce Your Tax Burden . . . 47
   Investing through a recession 50
   Three ways to reduce taxes
      through investments 51
   Inheriting investments means
      inheriting a tax burden 54
   Building family wealth with IRA
      Inheritance Trusts 56

7. Step 3: Be Smart With Business Assets 57
        Wise business structures and elections 59
        Buy-sell agreements for partnerships 62
        Key tax deductions for businesses. 65
        What's ahead for business taxes 67

8. Step 4: Reduce Your Estate Taxes. 69
        Are you a target of the federal estate tax?. 71
        Estate tax in Illinois and other states 75
        Three ways to reduce your estate tax burden 76

9. Tax Benefits of a Trust Vs. a Simple Will . . . 81

10. An Estate Plan Saves You More Than Taxes . 87
        Incapacitation is a very real issue 89
        Probate is a four-letter word 94
        Private matters should stay private 97
        There's no crystal ball for divorce
            and remarriage 101

11. How Not to Make It Work 107
        The cost of doing it yourself 109
        The cost of having no conductor 113
        The cost of not including family in decisions 114

Conclusion 118
Appendix/Online Resources 119
Tax and Estate Planning Glossary of Terms 120
Index 128
About the Authors 131
Request a Free Consultation 135
Order Copies of *Cut Your Tax in 2010* 136

Author Accolades

"Dean's knowledge and expertise is at the top of the scale."
—Dennis Duffy, estate planning attorney, Davenport, Iowa

"Anthony has uncovered the key to preserving wealth: you're never too young to get smart about estate planning. I'm working hard to build a legacy right now. There's no one I trust more than Anthony to help me preserve it."
—Jason Colton, CPA, Chicago, Illinois

"Anthony is a very bright attorney and does a great job for his clients. He also has a great personality. I recommend that any family take his advice on preparing their estate plan."
—Rial Moulton, estate planning attorney, Spokane, Washington

"Dean is one of the most talented estate planners and financial advisors that I know. He has the ability to understand complicated issues and reduce them to plans that work. He is brilliant."
—Dan Morris, estate and business planning attorney, Phoenix, Arizona

"My tax issues are complicated. My business requires frequent travel and I enjoy making unconventional investments in the financial markets. Anthony has always been ahead of the game when it comes to identifying tax opportunities that less astute advisers will miss. Take his tax advice and you'll be better off. It's really that simple."
—Erich Doerr, business consultant, Chicago, Illinois

"Dean is an outstanding attorney and well respected in the legal community. His knowledge and skill of estate planning, elder law, and tax planning is amazing."
—Charles Pyke, estate planning and elder law attorney, Stockbridge, Georgia

Acknowledgements

We would like to thank our families and our wives in particular, Peggy Perrelli and Sandy Hedeker, for their unending love and support. We'd also like to thank our staff for using our passion and knowledge of tax planning and estate planning to help empower our clients. And to our loyal clients, who inspire us every day.

This book wouldn't have been possible without LuAnn Glowacz, who orchestrated our passionate insights into eloquent, clever, and thought-provoking copy.

Additionally, we would like to thank others who have contributed to the development of this book: Thom Singer, Dave Morris, Elena Bazini, and Raquel Orsini.

Introduction

Both of my parents are immigrants to the United States. My father first lived in a tiny 400-square-foot home in Italy with eight family members. My mother's parents were factory workers in Poland. From those humble beginnings, my parents worked tirelessly to build family wealth from the ground up. My law partner and co-author, Dean Hedeker, shares a similar background to my parents. He started working at 12 years old delivering newspapers, and continued to diligently work his way through college to make ends meet. Today, both Dean and my father are successful businessmen who have provided for their children in ways that far surpass their own modest beginnings.

My generation is a product of their hard work. My life has been blessed with little compromise and financial sacrifice. For my first high school job, my wage per hour was more than what my grandmother was making when she retired. I attended the colleges of my choice. I chose the career path I wanted. I have a beautiful home and I drive a nice car. All of this was possible through the foundation that my parents and grandparents laid for me. Now that I am getting older, generating my own wealth, and having children of my own, I have a better understanding of the sacrifices my family made to ensure that my siblings and I started climbing toward success at a higher rung on the financial ladder than they did.

We will all play two very important roles in our lives when it comes to our family's financial legacy. The first role is as a provider. Many of us feel a basic responsibility to improve the financial situation we were born into and ensure that our children are better off than we were. My hope is that *Cut Your Tax in 2010* will help you understand how to protect and pass on your hard-earned money to make this happen. It's then your responsibility to seek the help of a professional to put a plan in place that fits your needs.

The second role you will play in your lifetime is that of a benefactor. This role comes with just as much financial responsibility as the first. It's been said that family wealth is rarely sustained beyond the third generation. Chances are, your grandchildren—and certainly your great-grandchildren—will inherit very little of your family's current wealth if you do not put the proper measures in place. Take a proactive role in helping your aging parents set up a smart, tax-efficient estate plan if they don't already have one. And educate your children about your family's finances and the responsibility they have as benefactors to protect that money for generations to come, as well as to use it to catapult their own financial successes.

Don't underestimate how a simple misunderstanding of changing tax laws can permanently handicap a family's financial future.

Anthony R. Perrelli, MBA, JD

There are several self-help financial gurus out there who have legitimately helped many of us create wealth by teaching us to work hard and save diligently. But that has created a mini-epidemic of average, hard-working people holding the bag on some huge taxes. The roadmap ended at building wealth and didn't include how to preserve it just as diligently.

It's for this reason that being a CPA or a lawyer was not enough for me. Some would call it being an overachiever, but that's really not my motivation. I have always believed the value of money is that it can create security. That's only true, however, if you look at your complete financial picture as a whole so that conflicts between making, saving, and passing on your wealth can be eliminated.

That's why I built a practice that integrates financial management, estate planning, tax planning, and tax preparation services under one roof. It's not an easy road, but it was the only road my heart would allow me to choose. I'm the only estate planner I know who works 18-hour days during tax season. And I'm one of only a handful of wealth managers who is equally concerned about the future financial health of my clients' grandchildren as I am for my clients' own financial health right now. I truly believe that your money is your legacy. And by treating it as such, you must take a holistic approach to preserving it by creating a seamless financial safety net throughout your lifetime and beyond.

One common thread binding these financial silos together is taxes. Taxes exist at every stage of building, maintaining, and passing on your wealth. My law partner and co-author, Anthony Perrelli, and I are passionate about preserving family legacies and including tax planning as a primary tool to accomplish it. We wrote **Cut Your Tax in 2010** to help lead you in the direction of mindfully managing your wealth and paying only the taxes that are necessary so that the rest can be used to fund your family's dreams now and in the future.

Dean R. Hedeker, CPA, RFC, JD

CHAPTER 1

Reasons to Rethink What You're Doing

"Potentially we've got trillion-dollar deficits for years to come, even with the economic recovery that we are working on."

–President Barack Obama

There may be a perfect storm brewing when it comes to your taxes this year. First, the government desperately needs to raise cash. Second, there are tax advantages available this year alone that only those paying close attention will benefit from. Third, some big changes may happen in your life this year—planned or unplanned, good or bad—that could throw your financial picture off balance and leave you owing more in taxes than you anticipated.

Uncle Sam needs your money now

There is no question that Uncle Sam needs your money this year. The U.S. stock market has just gone through the worst 10-year period in history, involving two separate market crashes in 2000-2002 and 2008-2009. We all know what happened next: the losses during this period surpassed those of the Great Depression. The real estate industry collapsed, which led to shortfalls in nearly every other industry over the subsequent months. What were we left with? The U.S. budget deficit hit a record $1.4 trillion in fiscal year 2009.

Take a close look at that last sentence. We said $1.4 *trillion*. That's a lot of money. In fact, our minds aren't equipped to easily comprehend such a number. David Schwartz, author of the children's book *How Much Is a Million?* conceptualized a "trillion" for *Time Magazine* readers in the January 2009 article "How to Understand a Trillion-Dollar Deficit":

> "One million seconds comes out to be about 11½ days. A billion seconds is 32 years. And a trillion seconds is 32,000 years," Schwartz explained. "I like to say that I have a pretty good idea what I'll be doing a million seconds from now, no idea what I'll be doing a billion seconds from now, and an excellent idea of what I'll be doing a trillion seconds from now."

And that's just the federal government. What about state government?

Our home state of Illinois is in particularly bad shape. Mike Flannery of CBS 2 Chicago reported in October 2009 that "the State of Illinois' pile of unpaid bills has grown to a record-breaking $3 billion. Comptroller Dan Hynes said ... it's never before been this bad at this point in any previous fiscal year."

Contributing to this deficit is a staggering loss of revenue from corporate income tax, personal income tax, and sales tax. This leads to a

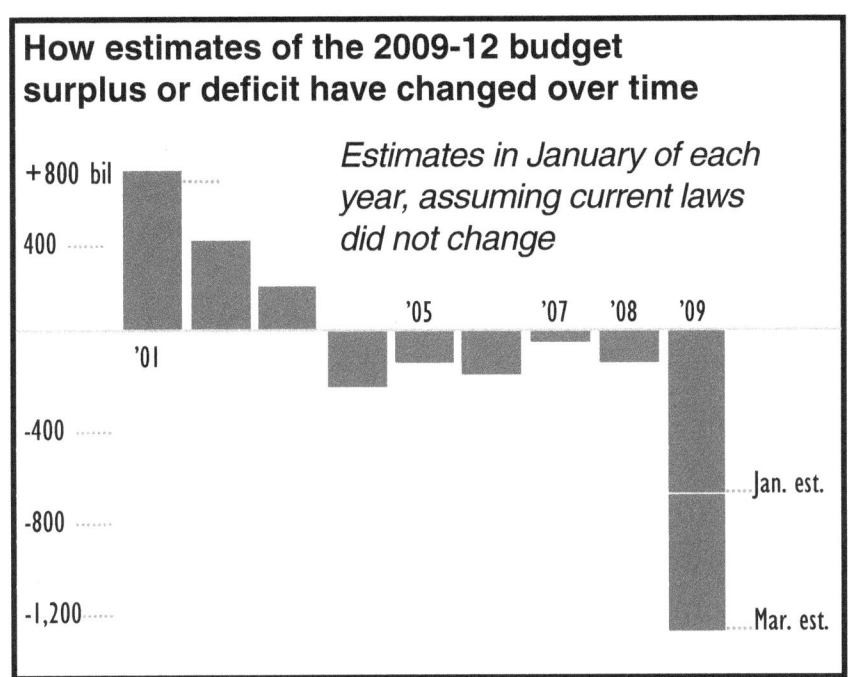

Congress had high hopes in 2001, predicting an $800 billion surplus from 2009 to 2012. By March 2009, Congress faced the reality of a trillion dollar deficit instead.

vicious cycle of having to raise taxes that more and more people are not generating the income to pay. These people are turning to government loans that aren't there. And the cycle continues. By the last quarter of 2009, it was reported that the State of Illinois was an average of three months behind on paying its own creditors.

For this reason, Illinois may see an income tax increase of 50 percent over the next year. This plan, publicly acknowledged by Governor Pat

Quinn in March 2009, would raise income tax from 3 percent to 4.5 percent.

Illinois isn't the only state in dire straits. The State of California made headlines in 2009 by handing out IOUs to creditors instead of actual money from July until September to avoid running out of cash (as reported by *Bloomberg.com* last September).

The bottom line is that while you may be hurting due to the recent economy bust, so are the federal and state governments. It's not only your well that's dry, it's every well in America. Somebody needs to shoulder an even greater responsibility for fixing that mess. Uncle Sam would like it to be you.

We're not insinuating that you should bail on your patriotic responsibility to pay taxes. But we are offering ideas to reduce that tax burden, by showing you ways to pay no more than is necessary.

Tax advantages in 2010

Every year that goes by is one year closer to (or further into) retirement. And every year there are new and different ways to plan for retirement. These tax and savings opportunities come and go, and missing one could cost you.

If you are retiring in 2010, you have a golden opportunity that retirees in 2009 did not have. That opportunity has to do with Roth IRAs, which we will cover more in depth later in this book. In 2010, everyone qualifies for Roth IRA conversion, regardless of income. And only in 2010 can you spread your tax responsibility over a two-year period. The bottom line is that if you are retired and have money still tied up in a former employer's 401k, you should seriously consider reinvesting that money this year or you will sorely miss out.

This year may also be a great time to sell real estate and pay capital gains taxes. Yes, that's what we said: you have a good opportunity to *pay* taxes this year. That's because capital gains taxes will increase in the years to come (remember the predicament Uncle Sam is facing right now). Also, if you were one of the many who experienced a noticeable dip in income lately, that dip could offset the capital gains taxes you would face when selling property or other **assets**. This is a tricky area, so please enlist the guidance of your tax adviser to determine if the opportunity applies to you.

Every plan needs maintenance

This may be the year for other substantial changes as well: the birth of a new grandchild, a divorce in the family, a shocking medical diagnosis. Each situation—whether good or bad—presents a new area of stress on your legacy. When life changes occur, it's time to re-evaluate and update your financial plan and **estate** documents to ensure that your ever-evolving wishes are properly addressed.

We'll be talking more about reducing your tax burden when facing certain life changes throughout this book. What we want to address right now is the importance of keeping a fluid process in place that can evolve as your family situation changes. We're not talking about changes that should happen eventually or in the next five years. We're talking about real-time changes in 2010. No one has a crystal ball. You'll never know with certainty when the clock will run out on ensuring that the legacy you imagine for your family becomes a reality.

Reviewing and making changes to your estate documents and investment portfolio every year can help ensure that any tax and personal changes that have occurred are addressed appropriately. In estate-planning terms, we call this a *maintenance program*. It can be set to renew with little effort on your part. An outdated plan that isn't taking advantage of current tax laws is not worth the investment you originally put into it.

CHAPTER 2

You're Richer Than You Think

"Over and over again the Courts have said that there is nothing sinister in so arranging affairs as to keep taxes as low as possible. Everyone does it, rich and poor alike ... for nobody owes any public duty to pay more than the law demands."

–Judge Learned Hand

You didn't dine on caviar while breakfasting from your yacht this morning, but the government doesn't care. Uncle Sam still thinks you're rich. That's because the government doesn't look at your cash the same way you do.

Why Uncle Sam thinks you're rich

When was the last time you really took stock of your assets? You may be surprised when you do. Make a simple list of them and then add them up. Here's an example:

- IRA, 401k: $700,000
- Brokerage (investments): $300,000
- Life Insurance: $200,000*
- Property (your home): $600,000
- CDs/Savings/Bank Accounts: $200,000
- Annuities: $100,000
- TOTAL: $2.1 million

* *Consider the death benefit of your life insurance, not the cash value.*

All of a sudden, you may realize you're a multi-millionaire after all. Congratulations!

But then why don't you feel rich? Because that's not free money; it's money you earned through blood, sweat, and tears. And it's money that you don't have easy access to because it is tucked into investments and assets. This creates a psychological barrier for most people that prevents them from spending their money foolishly. There are two well-known sayings that come to mind to help explain this point:

1. "People usually drink the milk from the cow rather than slaughter the cow." In other words, if you have a bank account worth $500,000 that is paying 2 percent interest, you will try to live on the 2 percent rather than touch the $500,000.

2. "The wealth that the kids receive is far more than the wealth you give up." That's because people look at their bank accounts and their investments alone as their **net worth**. They are more emotionally connected to house value and life insurance and often overlook the true financial value of those assets.

There will be times that you need to use these investments for important purposes: as much needed retirement support or as emergency funds to help children or grandchildren.

However, your reason for withdrawing is not usually a concern to the government. Whenever you cash out your assets, the government considers it money in your pocket.

Change the way you view your money

We can't necessarily blame Uncle Sam for thinking this way. For all the government knows, you may as well be withdrawing that money on a wild weekend in Vegas. And if you're going to throw that money away, Uncle Sam would like a share of it first. Plus, a good portion of that money is investments that have appreciated over time. That money hasn't been taxed yet. You can bet the government doesn't like the idea of you "wasting" money that has yet to be taxed.

There's good news, though. The government isn't entitled to as much of your money as you have been willing to share. It is well within your rights to structure your assets so that you can withdraw and use your own money tax free. Prove to the government that you're responsible with your money and the government will let you keep more of it.

Divide your money and earmark it for:

1. You (and your spouse)

2. Your future

3. Your legacy (kids and grandkids)

By doing this, you are essentially dividing that money into silos. Each silo contains a stockpile of funds for different benefactors at different times, thereby reducing your tax burden. Some of it you can use now or in the near future to fund your retirement or to cover other living expenses. Some of it can safeguard your future and be used as funding for disability or long-term health care. Plus, you'll want to set aside whatever you would like your children to inherit

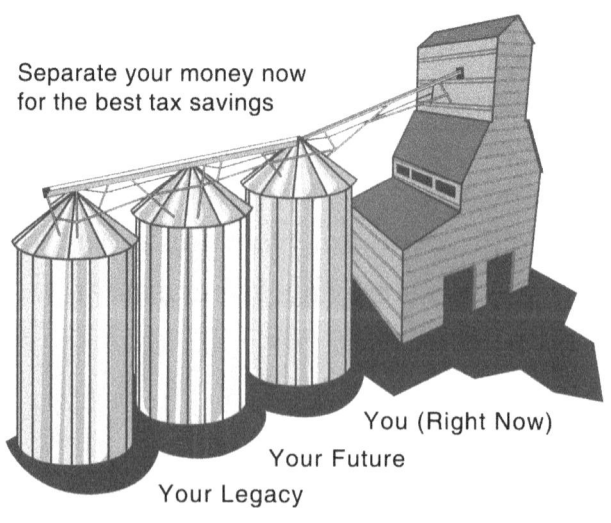

and, separately, what you would like to pass on directly to your grandchildren.

This isn't "playing the system." You're simply proactively organizing your estate using the best tools available. This book will give you the basic steps for how to do it.

CHAPTER 3

Capital Gains Trap

"People are always trying to find that magic way to not pay capital gains taxes. After all, capital gains taxes don't seem all that fair."

–Matt Kranz, USA Today

John and Emily Richards have been retired for five years. They own a quaint two-story home in suburban Chicago that they purchased in 1968 for $50,000. They aren't rich. John was an electrician and Emily served as a teacher for several years before leaving work to start a family. The couple experienced some hardships while raising their three girls, but they managed to pay off their home 11 years ago.

The Richards' tireless dedication to work and family paid off. Their modest home is now worth $575,000. And they have a substantial amount of savings and investments built up. They invested in rental property 20 years ago—a three-flat in Chicago. They even had the opportunity to purchase a vacation condo in Florida one year after they retired.

Now the Richards have three great real estate investments providing financial and lifestyle freedom for the couple in their retirement years. But within the next 20 years, these investments may also cost them. That's because, statistically speaking, John will likely pass away during that time. Emily will then be faced with some very key decisions on whether to sell some or all of the property in order to reduce the burden associated with real estate ownership. Her biggest financial obstacle will most likely be a hefty capital gains tax.

The problem with most retirement dreams is that they are often based on a joint vision of what the couple wants or needs. All too often, that dream turns into a significant physical and financial burden when one spouse passes away. One such burden is taxes.

Capital gains in a nutshell

We'll be referencing capital gains taxes throughout this book, but the subject deserves its own introduction. Here's why: capital gains taxes may be the most financially significant burden your beneficiaries will endure if you don't structure your estate properly.

Capital gains taxes don't apply to property alone. But they are a painfully common way large amounts of money are thrown away. If you'll be withdrawing long-term investments this year, you may be subject to capital gains taxes as well (even in this economy, many investments that were made decades ago are still worth substantially more than their purchase price).

When you owe capital gains taxes, the federal tax burden may be up to 28 percent of your gains. You'll also face a state capital gains tax, which varies a great deal. Illinois has a fairly simple rule of thumb: 3 percent tax on everything—whether it's a **capital gain** or not. Some would say that, although it's a simple rule, it's not necessarily fair.

Here's what the IRS has to say about capital gains and losses:

> *Almost everything you own and use for personal purposes, pleasure, or investment is a capital asset.*
>
> 1. *When you sell a capital asset, the difference between the amount you sell it for and your basis, which is usually what you paid for it, is a capital gain or a capital loss.*
>
> 2. *You must report all capital gains.*
>
> 3. *You may deduct capital losses only on investment property, not on property held for personal use.*
>
> 4. *Capital gains and losses are classified as long term or short term, depending on how long you hold the property before*

you sell it. If you hold it more than one year, your capital gain or loss is long term. If you hold it one year or less, your capital gain or loss is short term.

5. *Net capital gain is the amount by which your net long-term capital gain is more than your net short-term capital loss.*

6. *The tax rates that apply to net capital gain are generally lower than the tax rates that apply to other income and are called the maximum capital gains rates. (For 2010, the maximum capital gains rates are 0, 15, 25, or 28 percent, depending on a person's tax bracket.)*

7. *If your capital losses exceed your capital gains, the excess can be deducted on your tax return, up to an annual limit of $3,000 ($1,500 if you are married filing separately).*

8. *If your total net **capital loss** is more than the yearly limit on capital loss deductions, you can carry over the unused part to the next year and treat it as if you incurred it in that next year.*

*Source: IRS.gov: IRS TAX TIP 2009-35

Notice that capital losses can offset your capital gains in certain situations. If you lose money on a rental property, or if you lose your job and are unable to pay your bills, you may be able to avoid a certain amount of capital gains taxes.

Alternative Minimum Tax

Good old Uncle Sam doesn't let a lot of people off the hook. He's an opportunist, so he wisely introduced an alternative minimum tax (AMT) in 1970, which taxes just about any income that has otherwise fallen through the cracks.

When it comes to capital gains, short-term gains are taxed at ordinary income rates (which are much higher than capital gains taxes). And if there are too many long-term capital gains, they can be taxed at alternative minimum tax (AMT) rates, which are currently between 26 and 28 percent.

Work with your tax adviser to identify any potential AMT taxes you could face and how to avoid them by paying a lesser tax.

But determining what circumstances qualify can be tricky business so it's best to navigate that road with the help of a tax adviser.

Back to the Richards

Couples like the Richards usually own their homes through **joint tenancy,** which means that they hold the title on the property together. This allows one spouse to inherit the entire property without a court proceeding when the other spouse dies. This is a great idea in theory but it may come with huge tax consequences, especially for property that has appreciated over time like the Richards' family home. In certain states, joint tenancy may cause tax problems when one or both of the joint tenants die, depending on the size of the estate.

The problem with avoiding joint tenancy, however, is that you rarely know who will pass away first. There is a benefit of keeping the property ownership under the sole name of the family's breadwinner (John, in this case). But it is only the best choice if that individual dies first. This is because of a process called a *step-up in basis* or a readjustment of the base value of an appreciated asset. *Investopedia.com*, a website dedicated to financial education, explains step-up in basis this way:

> *In most cases, when an asset is passed on to a **beneficiary**, its value is more than what it was when the original owner acquired it. The asset therefore receives a step-up in basis so that the beneficiary's capital gains tax is minimized—because it is not based on the increase in value from the original purchase price.*

With joint tenancy, only half of the property will be stepped up when John dies. Emily's half will face capital gains taxes when she sells the property. But if the property is under John's name, the full value will be stepped up to today's value when Emily inherits it, reducing her capital gains burden significantly (or perhaps entirely). However, as we stated earlier, these tax benefits will only emerge if John dies first. And there are also potential **probate** issues with the ownership of property in one sole name as well.

The government has tried to reduce the tax burden of joint tenancy, but it requires the surviving spouse to act relatively quickly. If a married couple has lived in a home for more than two years, the first $500,000 of capital gains when the house is sold is not taxed ($250,000 for single owners). Since a step-up in basis happened at John's death when the house was valued at $575,000, that would exclude capital gains on all but $25,000 on the Richards' family home. But the rule only applies for two years after the asset is inherited.

In our experience, widows in Emily's situation rarely choose to sell their home within two years of a spouse's death. That home offers a sense of normalcy and security during the grieving process. Usually, it's only after the tax-free window of opportunity has closed that the surviving spouse is ready to move on.

If Emily waits to sell the house after the two-year period has passed, then the most gain she can exclude is $250,000. So if Emily sold the house for, say, $600,000 three years after John died, she would pay capital gains tax on a gain of $37,500.

The capital gains basis of the house for sale purposes is based on half of the value of the house at the time John died ($287,500) and half of the value of the house when it was originally purchased ($25,000). After subtracting Emily's $250,000 exclusion, we arrived at our total, which is a bigger tax burden than if John had been the sole owner of the home (in which case, the entire value of the house could have received a step-up in basis, reducing the capital gains significantly). If Emily passed away first, however, joint tenancy would be valuable.

So you see, it's important for you to go over your own scenarios with a tax adviser to determine what type of home ownership makes sense for you and your loved ones.

What about the Richards' other properties?

A **Section 1031 Exchange** may help reduce a portion of Emily's tax burden. Capital gains taxes can be deferred by exchanging one investment property for another. This is a viable option for people who own investment or business property.

The Richards' Chicago rental property may qualify for this type of exchange as an investment property (which means that Mr. and Mrs. Richards could not have used it for their own personal use). Emily could exchange the rental property for investment property closer to home (perhaps a lakefront property). Her children could then inherit it upon Emily's death, get a complete step-up in basis and pay no capital gains tax as long as they sell it for what it is worth when Emily passes away. After Emily's death, they could have the option of then using it as their vacation home and have a cost basis equal to the date of death value.

There may also be an opportunity to exchange the property for a **Real Estate Investment Trust (REIT)**, an option also known as a 1031-721 exchange. The IRS does not make REIT exchanges easy and there are some muddy guidelines surrounding it, but a tax adviser can help you sort through your specific options.

Alternatively, Emily could hold onto the property but let go of her heavy responsibilities by withdrawing some equity (cashing out some assets or refinancing) and hiring a management firm to handle maintenance and administration.

If the Florida condo had been used by the family as a vacation home, there are very few tax advantages for Emily. A vacation or second home generally does not qualify for a 1031 exchange and, at the same time, the $500,000 capital gains exception cannot be applied. Tax-wise, a **trust** would provide the only real benefit for the Richards family in this case. However, if the Richards family had not started using the Florida condo for personal use, and were renting or leasing the property instead, then the condo could qualify for the same tax options as the Chicago rental property (a 1031 Exchange or REIT).

Let's not overlook the fact that selling the rental property and Florida condo—and paying the applicable taxes—is a viable option. That's because, as we discussed in Chapter 1, capital gains taxes will increase significantly in 2011. Sometimes if selling is really what you want to do, then taking the tax hit sooner rather than later might be the best option.

What you should do

If you suspect that capital gains may be an issue for you or your beneficiaries, talk to a tax adviser about:

- What property you own and how much it has appreciated.
- Whether you intend to sell your property in the next five to ten years.
- Who will inherit your property when you die, and if they will sell it right away.
- What other investments may potentially be subject to capital gains taxes in the future.

The one absolute step for everyone facing major capital gains is to make sure you have a **Survivor's Trust** and **Family Trust** in place to shelter those assets from unnecessary tax burdens. We'll talk more about trusts in Chapters 9 and 10.

Chapter 4

Protect Your Assets in 4 Steps

"These unhappy times call for the building of plans that build from the bottom up."

–Franklin D. Roosevelt

There are endless ways to spend and save your money. Everyone's got a theory on the best way to do it, from *Rich Dad, Poor Dad* to *The Millionaire Next Door*. Much of the advice out there is good. Some of it is not so good.

The problem that we see with even the most popular tax advice out there is that it is focused on immediate gratification. The question being answered is, "What will work right now, to reduce my tax burden this year?" Good solutions focus on retirement and making your money stretch to serve you throughout your lifetime. While that's good planning, it isn't great. As estate planning attorneys, we just don't believe that making your money stretch to provide for you alone is enough. We think on a much broader scale. Your money is your legacy.

We happen to know that there are four basic steps that not only help you save and grow your money, but that can reduce your tax burden as well. Follow these steps and you (and your family) could save tens of thousands of dollars in taxes, depending on the size of your estate.

- Step 1: Convert to Roth IRAs
- Step 2: Invest to reduce your tax burden

- Step 3: Be smart with business assets
- Step 4: Reduce your estate taxes

These steps are explained in the next four chapters. They aren't the only solutions, but they are some hidden gems that can uncover a wealth of tax savings.

Chapter 5

Step 1: Convert to Roth IRAs

"Hundreds of dollars are sliding by for every day you put off funding a Roth IRA."

–Frugal Dad, personal finance blogger

We'll let you in on a highly guarded financial secret: Roth IRAs are a silver bullet when it comes to retirement savings. We're not exactly sure why Roth IRAs aren't touted more. But we certainly think they should be. If you plan on withdrawing money from your retirement accounts—whether for retirement, semi-retirement, or unemployment—we implore you to consider using Roth IRAs. That's because a Roth IRA:

- Can be a safer bet than keeping money in a 401k plan, especially if a large portion of that money is tied up in a previous employer's stock.

- Creates a legal "tax shelter" in which all of the growth on the money is tax free when you take it out after five years.

- Provides a tax-free conversion opportunity when you're facing a loss on your tax return and you convert that same amount from a traditional IRA to a Roth IRA.

As far as taxes go, traditional IRAs and Roth IRAs could not be more different. Traditional IRAs are extremely common but they are also ticking time bombs. Over time, a traditional IRA gets bigger and bigger while other less taxable assets like stock and bond investments, savings **bonds,** and annuities are often liquidated first. When it's time to withdraw money from the IRA, that money comes with a huge tax bill. Roth IRAs diffuse this bomb by sheltering long-term growth from taxation.

The beauty of recharacterization

Here's a brilliant point about Roth IRA conversions: you can undo them. There can be a hefty upfront tax cost associated with Roth IRA conversions—so what happens if you make the conversion and then lose money during the year? There is a tax strategy called a recharacterization that can help. Basically, a recharacterization can undo a Roth conversion. Simply put: you can act as if it never happened.

Money Magazine's Senior Editor Walter Updegrave raved about this option in a January 2009 "Ask the Expert" column, explaining that "it allows you to undo a conversion and transfer the balance (including earnings, if any) from your Roth IRA back to a traditional IRA. You can then leave it there or convert to a Roth IRA again later."

It is very rare in the world of taxation when you can literally change the numbers on your tax return the following year. But with Roth IRA conversions, it's possible.

2010: Year of the Roth IRA

Great news for you: 2010 is the year of the Roth IRA.

In 2009, you couldn't qualify for a Roth IRA conversion if your adjusted gross income exceeded $100,000 (even for couples). That made it difficult for many of us to proactively save tax-free dollars. But starting in 2010, anyone can qualify for a Roth conversion regardless of income. It's a little known fact with great benefits. According to a recent Natixis Global Associates survey, almost half of affluent American investors are unaware of this one-time opportunity in 2010 to convert tax-deferred retirement accounts into a Roth IRA.

Yes, you do pay taxes on the conversion, but Uncle Sam is giving you a break on that, too. If you convert to a Roth IRA in 2010, you can split the tax burden between your 2011 and 2012 tax returns. By paying your tax percentage (based on your tax bracket) over two years, your tax obligation is done. Every single dime of growth on that money can be withdrawn tax free. Even your beneficiaries can withdraw the remaining money tax free after you die. Sometimes Uncle Sam can be a nice guy after all.

Meet Sally Smith, semi-retiree

Let's put the benefits of a Roth IRA to the test with a little scenario:

> Sally Smith decided to quit her high-pressure consulting job at the age of 55 to pursue selling real estate as a sales agent, which offered her more flexibility and freedom. It was a move to semi-retirement of sorts. She is not alone in making that move. AARP reported in 2009 that many aging workers are switching to careers that come with less stress and more job satisfaction. But these jobs also carry with them less pay and fewer benefits (if any), which is a very risky scenario in today's economy. Sally made her career shift in 2007 initially and was quite successful. Then the bottom dropped out of the real estate market.

Due to these circumstances, Sally's shift to semi-retirement put her in ranks with what we consider the "under employed." She can no longer pay her bills on her income as a real estate professional. When Sally retired from full-time employment, she had approximately $300,000 in stocks, bonds, and bank accounts and had about $700,000 in traditional IRAs. By the end of 2009, she had the following income and expenses:

- $10,000 in dividends and interest
- $23,000 in business income
- ($74,000) in losses on stock sales
- ($10,000) in real estate taxes
- ($47,000) in home mortgage interest
- ($10,000) in medical expenses

This resulted in a $33,000 loss on her tax return. If she would have done nothing, she would have had difficulty getting any tax benefit for the loss. But by working with a tax adviser, she discovered three tax-saving options:

1. Pull $33,000 out of her IRA. This income would be offset by the loss, so it would not be fully taxed. But it would be subject to

a 10 percent penalty tax for withdrawing before the age of 59½.

2. Convert $33,000 from her IRA to a Roth IRA. This would also be tax free because the income from the conversion would be offset by the loss. But the additional benefit is that all of the growth on the $33,000 would be tax free as well. For example, if the market were to grow 50 percent in the next three years (in fact, the S&P 500 was up over 50 percent for a six-month period ending September 9, 2009), none of that income would be taxed; neither would the original $33,000.

3. Convert $33,000 to a Roth IRA plus an additional $33,000 for a total of $66,000. Since the second $33,000 more than offsets the loss, her taxable income would be $33,000 and the tax would be approximately $4,200 on the conversion.

Which option would you choose?

We prefer option three. There are taxes involved but, in this case, the benefit of converting more money into a Roth IRA is worth the expense. By converting $66,000 of IRA assets into a Roth

IRA, it becomes a legal "tax shelter" in which the entire $66,000 and all of its growth will never be taxed, if managed properly. So it's a way to create a tax-free source of income now. And, after paying a very minimal tax upfront, it creates an additional source of income that will be tax free when it is withdrawn.

Lost your job? Get a Roth IRA

We all know that it doesn't matter how close you are to retirement, you may still get that pink slip tomorrow.

When you suddenly find yourself with no income but with the same bills each month, what do you do? One option is to convert some traditional IRA money into a Roth IRA and pay no taxes on the conversion (because of your net operating loss for the year). If you don't already have an IRA, you can convert your existing 401k to a traditional IRA, then convert a portion to a Roth IRA for the same tax savings.

And as long as we're discussing unemployment, we urge you to please beware of the hidden fees associated with being jobless. One in particular: your unemployment benefits are taxable.

CHAPTER 6

Step 2: Invest to Reduce Your Tax Burden

"If past history was all there was to the game, the richest people would be librarians."

—Warren Buffett

There is no question that we are in a down market. Some experts are saying the worst is over, but only time will tell if that's true. If we have learned anything from the investment experts, it's that predicting the future based on what has happened before—and betting on that prediction—is risky.

Personal finance columnist Gail MarksJarvis wrote in her August 1, 2009, *Chicago Tribune* column, "Investors concerned about protecting their money in downturns are likely to be disappointed: A study of the most respected investment newsletters shows that the pros might have been right in one of the last two market crashes, but typically not both. And in the good times, they generally got it wrong too."

Now that we have this dismal news out of the way, what is the bright side?

When it comes to taxes, declaring capital losses on your investments can save you money during tax season by offsetting capital gains in other areas. Furthermore, there are ways to invest your money wisely whatever the economy may be. Investing your money remains a smart choice (as opposed to spending your money or stashing it in your mattress), as long as you invest intelligently for your own individual situation.

Investing through a recession

Financial advisers like co-author Dean Hedeker have learned several lessons during this recent recession. Perhaps most importantly, the standard philosophy of "buy and hold" failed this time around.

This strategy came about in the 1970's as a very simplified aspect of the Fama-French model, a long-term investment strategy based on the theory that financial markets will produce a good rate of return in the long run, despite periods of volatility. This strategy worked extremely well for decades (and will probably work well again). But it failed recently because, as it turns out, investors are not as rational as we assumed they were. Many well-intentioned people took the "buy and hold" idea to an extreme and held onto poor investments longer than they should have.

Perhaps a better way to weather a modern recession is to "advance and protect." Investing in this economy is like gardening: you cannot simply plant a garden and watch it grow. You need to prune, pull weeds, and harvest continually to allow that garden to thrive.

The same is true when you invest: look for areas that will grow (higher risk) and then consider transferring that growth to areas that can better protect it (lower risk). Thus, the term "advance and protect."

Much of this comes down to re-examining risk parameters. For instance, investment advisers are reconsidering **money market accounts** as a legitimate investment alternative. Traditionally, if an investment adviser put a client's money into a cash account like a money market account, he wasn't doing his job because a cash account isn't a true "investment." But these days, cash is an acceptable—and an essential—asset class: it's one that protects a portion of your assets while your other investments receive a financial workout. The same idea rationalizes expanding beyond stocks and bonds and using other asset classes like real estate, commodities, and currencies to balance a portfolio.

Three ways to reduce taxes through investments

1. **Tax-free municipal bonds:** This investment (which can be low risk) is often overlooked. That's because interest on regular bonds are taxed at traditional income tax levels

instead of the lower stock dividend tax levels. But municipal bonds are different. *Kiplinger's Personal Finance* spilled the beans on this little secret in 2008 when the magazine reported that "...bond investors have an escape not available to stock owners. They can buy municipal bonds and pay no federal taxes at all on the interest. And if you buy muni bonds from in-state issuers, you can avoid state and local taxes as well."

Municipal bond investors, however, need to consider the alternative minimum tax (AMT), which we introduced in Chapter 3. Certain types of municipal bonds may create or increase their exposure to AMT.

2. **Stocks (capital gains assets):** Stock gains are considered capital gains, and since long-term capital gains tax rates are significantly less than regular interest rates (a difference of 10 percent or more), stocks are a great tax reducer. For example, if you've seen capital losses on certain stocks, sell up to $3,000 before the end of the year. You will be able to declare that as capital loss on your tax forms.

3. **Roth IRA conversions:** You may be starting to notice that we're fans of Roth IRAs. They deserve a mention here, too. Roth IRAs are a form of investment, after all, and they are terrific tax shelters.

   Roth IRA conversions were a golden opportunity for capital loss sufferers who were smart enough to jump onto them in 2009. As we pointed out earlier, these IRAs can potentially generate a significant amount of tax-free income. Remember that the S&P 500 was up over 50 percent in the 6-month period ending September 9, 2009. A person over 50 years of age who had the maximum $6,000 for the year invested in a Roth IRA during that time experienced $3,000 in tax-free growth.

   When holding on to investments for more than 20 years is an option, investing in an employer's 401k program, traditional IRAs, and a new home are still three excellent ways to grow wealth for the future. These assets are free of income tax and capital gains tax until you're ready to use them further down the line.

Inheriting investments means inheriting a tax burden

We've never met a client who isn't worried that they may deplete their assets before they die. It's commendable to be concerned about your personal finances in this way. But we'd like to put your mind at ease: statistically speaking, you will not spend your life savings before you die. It's very hard to do.

So the next question is: how will your investments affect your beneficiaries?

Some of our most mature clients hold vivid memories of the Great Depression. That experience, coupled with the recent market volatility, has taught them how untrustworthy the stock market can be. For instance, we often meet widows who are heavily invested in traditional savings bonds alone.

Here's a very common scenario:

> Greta is an 89-year-old widow who owns several savings bonds. She is in the 15 percent tax bracket. Her children, however, have built additional wealth and success for themselves and are in the higher 25 percent tax bracket.

When Greta's savings bonds pass on to her children and they cash them in, all of the income (let's say it grew 4 percent) will be taxed. Greta's children will pay nearly double the taxes that she would have paid.

Perhaps Greta should have cashed in the savings bonds and paid the tax in her lower tax bracket. Or she could have invested in tax-free municipal bonds instead.

When you buy and hold even low-risk investments for the purpose of passing those investments on to your children, stop to consider the tax burden you'll be handing them as well. It's the American dream for kids to be more successful than their parents. But that also means that the kids are subject to more taxes than their parents as well.

This is simply food for thought. Everyone's investment portfolio is different so it's impossible to dispense general advice that will work for everyone. The main point to this chapter: make sure your investments are wise not only for growth purposes but for tax purposes as well. And consider who may be the best person to bear the tax burden on that growth: you or your beneficiaries.

Building family wealth with IRA Inheritance Trusts

When it comes down to it, you don't just want to reduce your beneficiaries' tax burden on investments. What you really want to do is to help build your family's wealth. One way to accomplish both is with an IRA Inheritance Trust® for grandchildren.

IRA Inheritance Trusts enable traditional and Roth IRAs to grow tax deferred or tax free well past the original owner's lifetime. Minimum distribution requirements apply, which means the beneficiary is required to withdraw a certain amount each year. But these are based on the beneficiary's estimated life expectancy. Think of an IRA Inheritance Trust as a supercharger for your IRA. For a grandchild that is currently 20 years old, for example, that life expectancy may be around 80 years of age.

Transferring IRA money to a grandchild slows down the tax process. And, by skipping your children (no offense to your children), you are creating a legitimate tax shelter that has the potential to span close to a century of growth.

CHAPTER 7

Step 3: Be Smart With Business Assets

"The hardest thing to understand in the world is the income tax."

–Albert Einstein

Many of our clients are business owners just like us. Owning your own business has many advantages, but taxes are not one of them. Whether you work alone, in a partnership, or as a fearless leader of many, the tax implications of running a business can be substantial. But there are ways that you can cut your tax burden this year and beat Uncle Sam at his own game.

Wise business structures and elections

A **sole proprietorship** is the most common business structure for individuals just starting out in self employment. It's the easiest and least expensive structure to set up. But it is also the most costly business structure when it comes to taxes because sole proprietors not only have to pay income tax but they also pay self-employment tax. Sole proprietorship comes with unlimited liability for the individual as well, which means business and personal assets are equally at risk.

Many self-employed individuals are scared off by the idea of "unlimited liability" and mixing business with personal risk. For that reason, a **Limited Liability Company (LLC)** structure is a common consideration. One of the benefits of an LLC is that an election can be taken allowing it to be treated as a corporation or a partnership for tax purposes. As a result, an LLC being treated as a partnership combines the limited liability features of a corporation with the tax efficiencies and operational flexibility of a partnership. But while the idea of limited liability is appealing, it's not as bulletproof as it sounds. Partnership earnings can be subject to self-employment tax just as sole proprietorship earnings are. And it can be more expensive to create an LLC than a partnership or sole proprietorship.

One alternative to a simple sole proprietorship, LLC, or partnership is for small business owners to elect a **Subchapter S Corporation (S-Corp)** distinction. An S-Corp is more of a tax election than an actual business structure. It can be valuable for self-employed individuals and growing businesses in which the owner is still very involved in day-to-day activities.

According to the IRS, approximately 4 million businesses have elected S-Corp status. It offers protection against personal liability, and income and gains are taxed only once. Historically, S-Corps experience a lower risk of being audited than sole proprietors as well. That's because when you operate your business as an S-Corp, partnership, or LLC, income and expenses are "passed through" to you on your personal tax return. The key, however, is to pay yourself a reasonable salary if you do elect S-Corp status. If you had been making $80,000 as a sole proprietor but then decide to give yourself a take-home salary of $12,000 under an S-Corp (to reduce your tax burden), eyebrows at the IRS will be raised.

Another relatively new approach is to create an LLC, elect for it to be treated as a corporation, and then have the LLC elect S-Corp status. This S-LLC status combines the tax benefits of an S-Corp with the asset protection planning of an LLC.

We believe some form of S-Corp election is an important consideration for most business owners with the exception of those who run businesses that are heavily invested in business capital (primarily as equipment). These are usually manufacturers who routinely reinvest in their business by purchasing and maintaining machinery and other necessary supplies and equipment.

A **Subchapter C Corporation (C-Corp)** distinction is useful for capital-intensive businesses like these because the first $50,000 of income is taxed at a corporate rate of 15 percent, whereas the owners of the business may be taxed at higher rates. The concern about C-Corp status is that there is a potential for double taxation when dividends are distributed to shareholders (when the business owner pays himself). But with a capital-intensive business, most income is directly reinvested into the business and therefore only gets subjected to the one lower tax.

Buy-sell agreements for partnerships

When running a business with a partner, a buy-sell agreement is crucially important. In fact, it's been called a "business will" for business partners and shareholders. While this is not necessarily a tax issue, overlooking its importance can have devastating consequences for a business. Here's an example:

> Three Cappelli brothers own a family restaurant together in Chicago, which they inherited from their parents. The brothers are equal partners in the business and have each fallen into roles within the business that suit their talents and have allowed the restaurant to thrive. Each brother is married and has three children—and each dreams of one day passing the family

business down to them (with or without the children's returned enthusiasm for the idea).

Over the next two decades, the brothers pass away one by one, leaving their wives to inherit and run the restaurant. As their wives pass away, each of the three children inherit one third of their parents' original portion of the restaurant. Within a generation's time, the restaurant has gone from three to 12 owners, each with varying degrees of interest, capability, and determination to ensure the restaurant's continued success.

What will happen to the restaurant? Experience tells us that it will become so fraught with disorganization and conflict that it will fail completely.

This problem doesn't just plague family businesses. Perhaps you own a professional services business like we do. Taking on a partner can be a great way to grow the business. But what happens when that partner passes away and his or her assets pass on to the spouse or children? Our wives are smart (perhaps even smarter than we are) but they wouldn't want—

nor would they legally be allowed—to run the law firm if one of us passed away.

The easy fix here is a buy-sell agreement funded with life insurance. Each year, the business partners either calculate or hold a meeting to determine the present value of the business (usually a formula based on earnings or gross revenue). If something happens to one partner, it is predetermined that the other partner(s) will purchase the benefactor's inherited share of the business at the currently set cost. When this buy-sell agreement is funded with life insurance, the surviving partner(s) can use that insurance to pay for any buyout necessary. This gives the partners and their beneficiaries a mutually beneficial resolution to maintaining the future integrity of the business.

The buy-sell agreement also covers first right of refusal to buy out a partner's share of a business if that other partner decides to sell.

Key tax deductions for businesses

The amount of tax write-offs available to business owners is staggering. But most of us fail to take advantage of these allowances because it's yet another process to add to our daily business routines. We implore you to utilize the business tax advantages that Uncle Sam has allowed for you. Your tax percentage will noticeably decrease. Here are some tips for 2010 that you may not know about, edited from information we provide annually to our own clients.

1. Speed up equipment write-offs by immediately deducting up to $250,000 of equipment costs and other business assets placed in service during the year.

2. Recheck the standard mileage rate annually.

3. Take "extra" tax credits for hiring certain disadvantaged workers.

4. Increase your home office deductions if you are self-employed and use part of your home exclusively as your principal place of business. (But please be reasonable on

the amount of space out of your home that you deduct. This is one of the top reasons businesses are audited.)

5. Take a small business deduction of up to $5,000 off the expenses you incur in starting up a new or sideline business, but only in its first year.

6. Recheck your depreciation calculation. Congress authorized a 15-year write-off period for qualified restaurants and leasehold improvements.

7. Don't forget the out-of-pocket business expenses of:

    - Legal and accounting fees.
    - Business telephone calls made away from your office.
    - Business supplies.
    - Business usage of personal computer expenses such as paper, printer, etc.
    - Interest on credit cards.
    - Home entertainment for business purposes.

- Online services used for business e-mail and research.
- Subscriptions to business publications.
- Dues for professional organizations.
- Various travel expenses, the dry cleaning of business clothes, and tips paid to doormen.
- Repairs to business equipment.
- Cell phone costs relating to business.

8. Know whether or not a **fringe benefit** is taxable income.

9. Recheck medical insurance premiums if you are self-employed.

10. Check to see if you can take a Net Operating Loss (NOL) carry-back.

What's ahead for business taxes?

The last two years ushered in important new tax laws for businesses. The Bush administration handed out plenty of checks in 2008, and 2009 brought us the year of the Obama economic stimulus package, which affected small business owners in a big way.

There's no doubt that the 2010 comprehensive tax package from the Obama administration will include more items of note for small businesses. You can stay on top of this news at *www.cutyourtax.com* throughout the year.

CHAPTER 8

Step 4: Reduce Your Estate Taxes

"In this world nothing can be said to be certain, except death and taxes."

–Benjamin Franklin

You certainly have heard this quote from Ben Franklin about death and taxes before. But you may not have considered that sometimes the two subjects—death and taxes—work together. It's called the **estate tax** (often nicknamed the death tax). And it's certainly one of the most important topics that we'll cover in this book.

The estate tax is an issue we battle every day because it affects the two main specialties of our law firm: tax planning and **estate planning**. The issue has been fraught with controversy and confusion, especially this year, so we think it's important to lay out the facts for you here.

Are you a target of the federal estate tax?

Essentially, an estate tax is applied to the taxable estate of a deceased person. The tax does not apply to everyone because we are all exempt up to a certain amount. In fact, the federal estate tax really only applies to 2 percent of the U.S. population.

But that doesn't mean that just the richest of the rich are subjected to it. You have enough wealth to be concerned about heavy taxation or you wouldn't be reading this book. This prequalifies you as a potential target of the estate tax in the coming years, both as a beneficiary and a benefactor.

For many years, the federal estate tax applied to anyone owning $1 million or more in assets. If you recall in Chapter 2, it doesn't take much for an average, hardworking family to acquire that much total wealth. In 2001, the Bush administration set out to gradually raise the tax exemption status to $3.5 million per person. The tax rate was also reduced from 55 percent to 45 percent. This relieved the burden of an estate tax for most of us.

Now comes the area of speculation and opportunity. The current estate tax was slated to expire in 2010 with the original exemption of $1 million (at a 55 percent rate) going into effect in 2011. That left 2010 as a potentially tax-free year (when it comes to federal estate taxes). Some started calling 2010 "the year to die" for this reason, but we knew this scenario was highly unlikely. By allowing the federal estate tax to expire for one year, the U.S. government would lose millions, if not billions, of much needed revenue. We all thought it was inconceivable that Uncle Sam would let that happen.

Still, in early December 2009, a decision had not been made by Congress. *The Washington Post* published that "unless something is done, 2010 will be the year to throw Mama from the train, tax-free. This would be terrible policy, not to mention unkind to Mama."

The editorial went on to recommend that the 2009 level not only be extended for one year, but that it be extended permanently so that those with estates straddling the line between $1 million and $3.5 million are spared that heavy tax burden that is scheduled to return in 2011.

And that's just what the House did. At the final hour in 2009, the House approved to not only extend the $3.5 million exemption limit through 2010, but they voted to make it permanent.

That decision did not sit well with the Senate, however. At the time this book was published, the Senate Democrats had failed to push even a short-term extension through. The *Wall Street Journal* reported in mid-December 2009 that, "Lawmakers already were promising…to revisit the issue early next year. One option is to pass a new tax retroactive to the beginning of 2010."

This Congressional mess is a nightmare for our clients because not having an estate tax in 2010 causes estates less than $3.5 million to be subject to capital gains taxation. And the potential of lawsuits due to a retroactive tax is imminent. It's essentially a train wreck.

Congress knew about this problem since the day the legislation was drafted in 1991, but yet they wait until the eleventh hour to deal with it. Even then, they still cannot agree on things. It presents a grim view of what will likely happen with Congress when a broader income, estate, and gift tax bill is debated.

Here's a summary of what the federal estate tax situation could mean for you:

- If the federal estate tax goes into effect retroactively, inheritors may be surprised with huge taxes that they cannot afford to pay.

- The repeal also affects generation-skipping transfer (GST) taxes and gift taxes, dramatically lowering the tax bill on giving money to grandchildren.

- Estates that escape a federal estate tax in 2010 may be faced with heavy capital gains taxes instead.

- As of today, the estate tax is still scheduled to be back with a vengeance in 2011, at only a $1 million exemption, which affects many more of us than ever before.

Given these complications, your current estate plan may now be unbalanced. And if you don't have an estate plan, your legacy is in more danger than ever because of these changes in exemptions.

To keep up with the current estate tax law situation, visit our website, www.cutyourtax.com.

Estate tax in Illinois and other states

Regardless of what happens with the federal estate tax, most states have their own estate taxes for you to worry about. Illinois' estate tax kicks in at $2 million, which is well below the current federal exemption. So even if you escape the current federal estate tax, you may not be off the hook in your own state. The exceptions to this rule are snow-bird-heavy states like Florida, Arizona, or Texas (these states have no additional estate tax).

Some states have very unfriendly estate tax rules when it comes to inheritors. Pennsylvania, for instance, has an **inheritance tax** that applies to all estates, regardless of size, depending on the value of the assets and the relationship of the beneficiary to the benefactor. Children and grandchildren are taxed more than spouses. Siblings are taxed more than children and grandchildren. And nieces and nephews are taxed more than siblings. Indiana has a similar inheritance tax structure. It's confusing and it's unfair to an individual who doesn't have a spouse or children.

Three ways to reduce your estate tax burden

According to the IRS, this is the "simple" explanation of what can be taxed as part of your estate:

> *"The Gross Estate of the decedent consists of an accounting of everything you own or have certain interests in at the date of death (Refer to Form 706). The **fair market value** of these items is used, not necessarily what you paid for them or what their values were when you acquired them. The total of all of these items is your 'Gross Estate.' The includible property may consist of cash and securities, real estate, insurance, trusts,*

annuities, business interests, and other assets. Keep in mind that the Gross Estate will likely include non-probate as well as probate property."

*(From IRS.gov's Frequently Asked Questions on Estate Taxes.)

Did you get that? In plain English, when the total assets you own when you die—money and property—exceed the estate tax exemption limit, you are subject to estate taxes on those assets based on **current market value**. "Current market value" is a key point that many folks—and their tax advisers—overlook. If you have assets that have appreciated (or depreciated) over time, you are taxed on the current value, not the price you paid originally.

When put into those terms, it seems pretty cut and dried. But there are still three important ways to reduce your estate tax burden by thousands of dollars.

1. **Trust in Revocable Living Trusts:** If you are married and your estate exceeds either the state or federal estate tax exemption, you could save hundreds of thousands of dollars in taxes by having Revocable

Living Trusts in place. (You won't save in taxes if you're single, but you will save probate and other costs.)

2. **Be a giver:** Gifting your money is a great option if you are only marginally over the estate tax exemption limit. Let's say you exceed the limit by $150,000. You can give that amount of money in separate $13,000 increments (the maximum per year allowance while remaining tax free) to family members—and even more to charitable organizations—to reduce your estate total before you pass away.

   This option is particularly useful if you become incapacitated and death is imminent (sounds horrible but it's true). The key to doing this is to include gifting instructions in your estate plan for the person you name as your **Power of Attorney.** That way, your wishes can be carried out—and your loved ones can avoid unnecessary taxes—even when you can no longer carry out these wishes yourself.

3. **Find out the valuation of your assets:** This is a key tip because it is often overlooked. There is a discount for lack

of marketability or lack of control that you should become familiar with if you own any property or business assets with another person.

The simple argument here is that your half of these jointly held assets are not actually *worth* half. No one will want to buy half of your home when you die because your spouse still owns the other half. The same is true with a business.

When you exceed the estate tax exemption by more than a margin, you still have options to reduce your tax burden. These options, however, are based on your individual situation and needs and are not one-size-fits-all.

Perhaps a **Family Limited Partnership** is an appropriate option. Or a **Grantor Retained Annuity Trust (GRAT)** might allow you to make substantial financial gifts to family members without paying a **gift tax**. Life insurance trusts, charitable giving, and dozens of other options might save you money as well. Simple deductions like the amount of your mortgage or other debts—even the administration cost to handle the affairs of your estate (including attorney fees)—should not be overlooked.

CHAPTER 9

Tax Benefits of a Trust Vs. a Simple Will

A Living Will is not a Simple Will

*You may have heard of a **Living Will**, which is not the same as a **Simple Will**.*

*While a Simple Will addresses your wishes after you die, a Living Will (which is a component of an **Advance Health Care Directive**) addresses your wishes while you are alive and have perhaps become incapacitated due to an injury, disease, or illness (an issue we will discuss in Chapter 10).*

Both types of wills are important components of an estate plan.

Creating a **will** is a part of growing up: you get married, buy a house, have kids ... create a will. Most of us have a **Simple Will** in place (if anything). A Simple Will is necessary to name custody of your children but when it comes to handling finances, a will is usually not enough.

We often call a Simple Will an "I love you" will. That's because we see it as more of a gesture of love than a smart stand-alone legal document. It basically states, "When I die, I leave everything to my wife. Or if she dies first, she'll leave everything to me." After all, that's what marriage is: an equal partnership, right?

Not if you want to protect your family's legacy.

If you have more than $500,000 in assets, simply leaving your spouse everything will leave them with a large mess to clean up when it comes to taxes, court fees, and more. Most Baby Boomers who own a house and have some retirement savings and other investments built up will easily surpass this threshold.

We've touched on a few tax benefits of an estate plan. But what is an estate plan? It's not a document itself but more of a customized series of documents designed to carry out your exact wishes when you become incapacitated or when you die. An estate plan can include a Simple Will but it also includes any combination of trusts, Power of Attorney designations, and other documents. When a solid estate plan is in place, you maintain control of your legacy well after you've passed away.

The biggest tax benefit that comes with having an estate plan is that it allows you to have a trust in place for distributing your wealth to your beneficiaries. The following scenario outlines the tax implications of a Simple Will alone versus a Survivor's Trust/Family Trust combination:

> Joe and Mary have about $4 million in assets, including a beautiful suburban Chicago home, a dry cleaning storefront that Joe built from the ground up 12 years ago, and several investments including an IRA and two mutual funds. They also have two children who are 13 and 15 years old.
>
> Like any responsible couple, Joe and Mary put together a Simple Will soon after their first child was born. Their main concern

was to name a guardian for the child if anything were to happen to both of them. They updated their will when their second child was 2 years old. But they haven't touched it since and they never supplemented the Simple Will with other important estate planning documents.

If Joe passes away first, Mary will inherit the entire $4 million that the couple earned. This will lead to huge estate taxes when she dies—taxes that her children will bear the burden of paying out of their inheritance. What's more, a Simple Will puts an estate directly into **probate** (a complication that we will discuss in Chapter 10). That's precious time and money that could put the family's business in jeopardy.

The following illustration shows a comparison of a Simple Will versus a trust, using Joe and Mary's family as the example. At the bottom, we estimated the price tag for each option. You'll see that while setting up trusts has an upfront cost, that price is much smaller than the price your family could potentially pay by relying on a Simple Will alone.

A Simple Will Vs. Trusts

A Simple Will

Joe passes away & leaves his half ($2 million) to Mary. Now Mary is "worth" $4 million.

$4 million

$4 million

Mary passes away several years later, splitting the assets evenly between her two adult children.

$4 million

Because of Mary's high net worth, her children are responsible for paying the following estimated taxes and fees*:

$200,000 Probate Expenses**
$235,000 Illinois Estate Tax
$30,000 Federal Estate Tax***

Trusts

$4 million

Joe passes away & his half ($2 million) goes into a family trust for Mary & the children. Mary's half ($2 million) goes into a survivor's trust. Mary has control over both trusts.

$2 million

$2 million

Mary passes away several years later, giving her children the assets in the survivor's trust. The family trust passes to the children separately.

$4 million

Since Mary's sole net worth remains at half the original estate total, her children are estimated to owe*:

$45k-$85k Administrator Expenses
$0 Federal & State Estate Taxes
$0 Probate Expenses

Simple Will
Starting assets = $4 million
Ending assets = **$3.535 million**

Trusts
Starting assets = $4 million
Ending assets = **$3.95 million**

Difference of more than $400,000

© Hedeker & Perrelli, Ltd.

* Estimated totals for an Illinois estate. Actual taxes & fees vary.
** Nolo estimates probate expenses (attorney and court fees) can cost up to 5 percent of an estate.
*** Based on 2009 rates, which may take effect retroactively.

CHAPTER 10

An Estate Plan Saves You More Than Taxes

"No one is useless in the world who lightens the burden of it for anyone else."

–Charles Dickens

This book is about taxes. But we're estate planning attorneys, too. So we can't imagine why you wouldn't want to know how to save time and money—beyond taxes alone—by having a solid estate plan. So while we won't dwell on these issues, we do want to introduce four additional reasons why estate planning is an excellent idea.

Incapacitation is a very real issue

The following story by co-author Dean Hedeker illustrates an all-too-common scenario:

> *Several years before I met my wife, Sandy, her mother was stricken with Alzheimer's disease. Sandy often talks about how terrifying it was to see her mother slowly lose herself over the span of seven years. Her long-term memory stayed sharp for some time. For example, she could describe the china pattern on the dishes she once owned but, at the same time, she couldn't remember to feed herself.*
>
> *In the last two years of her life, Sandy's mother was completely lost within herself— she couldn't communicate and she didn't*

recognize the people who loved her. It was heartbreaking. Sandy's mother was only 67 years old when she passed away.

As the illness was first progressing, Sandy started the process of acquiring control over her mother's assets. There were no trusts or guardianship documents in place so she needed to start from square one. It was a painfully difficult process and the guardianship proceedings were messy, to say the least. The most painful part, however, came with not knowing how her mother would have chosen to die. Life support and quality of life issues were never discussed when Sandy's mother was healthy.

These issues are added burdens that all too many of us needlessly face.

Alzheimer's Disease International recently revealed that 35 million people around the world are struggling with Alzheimer's. That's 10 percent more than experts originally thought. The Associated Press reports that, "Barring a medical breakthrough...dementia will nearly double every 20 years. By 2050, it will affect a staggering 115.4 million people."

What's more, the American Academy of Neurology reports that declining financial skills can be one of the first signs of Alzheimer's disease. And it can occur as much as a year before the disease is actually diagnosed. An unexplained decline in the ability to balance a checkbook or calculate a tip at a restaurant could be early warning signs.

Alzheimer's is a growing disease because it mostly affects people ages 65 and older. We're all living longer, so Alzheimer's disease is a very real threat to every one of us.

If you are blessed enough to escape the grasp of Alzheimer's, chances are you will not be left completely unscathed. The IBM Human Ability and Accessibility Center cites the following statistics: In 1950, there were 3,000 centenarians in the U.S. That number has risen to an estimated 55,000 today. By 2050, experts anticipate there will be 1 million centenarians (not to mention the vast amounts of people in their 80s and 90s).

The bottom line is that we will live a long time. So we all have a very strong chance of becoming incapacitated before we die. Unfortunately, we don't always get ample warning before it's too late to prepare for the worst.

As estate planning attorneys, we witness this scenario all too often. By the time a loved one is incapacitated, whether by Alzheimer's or another disability, they are no longer able to handle estate matters. The burden of making significant financial and health decisions falls onto loved ones. By this time, family members are often haunted by doubts: "Am I making the right decisions? Is this what my loved one would have wanted?"

When you eliminate those questions, you eliminate a huge obstacle your loved ones could face at the worst possible time. Estate planning helps do that through the following components:

1. **Incapacity Planning:** What safeguards do you have in place for when you are incapacitated? You can have much more control over what happens to you and your money than you may think. An Advance Health Care Directive, which includes **Health Care Power of Attorney,** Living Will, and **HIPAA authorizations,** can ensure that your wishes about your own health are heeded.

   And naming a Financial Power of Attorney, Disability Panel, and Disability Trustee can do the same for your assets.

2. **Living Trust:** Control what happens to your money before you can no longer make financial decisions. Trusts eliminate a "free for all" on your estate by allowing you to predetermine who has access to your money and how they can use it. Trusts also ensure that the details of your estate remain private and can spare your family from guardianship issues while you're alive, as well as probate issues after you're gone.

3. **Medicaid Roadmap:** Assets can quickly dwindle away when nursing home costs come into play. According to the Department of Health and Human Services, about half of all nursing home residents pay the costs out of their own savings. And "after these savings and other resources are spent, many people who stay in nursing homes for long periods eventually become eligible for Medicaid." Ouch.

So the government only wants to provide Medicaid when your well is bone dry. But it really doesn't need to come to that. Certain property, trust funds, and other assets cannot legally be touched. An estate plan can help you protect what is yours and put a plan in place to utilize Medicaid in a way that is appropriate for you.

It's important to note that health issues don't just occur when we get older. Special needs planning is also covered well by estate plans. In particular, a special needs trust gives parents and grandparents the ability to provide for a disabled child while allowing the child to remain eligible for government aid.

Probate is a four-letter word

Some lawyers love probate. We happen to think probate is a four-letter word. According to the legal advocacy organization Nolo, about 5 percent of a person's property can be spent by the time probate runs its course, which in some states (including Illinois), may take up to 2 years. That's $30,000 on a $600,000 home. It's a needless waste of time and money for you, for your family, and for the courts (which, of course, happen to be funded by your own tax dollars).

Probate occurs when you have assets titled in your name when you die. It is the process of changing ownership of these belongings to a beneficiary. Basically, when a deceased person has only a will or no formal final wishes at all, a probate proceeding will pay off creditors first and the family receives what's left. It's only fair to point out that probate is a rock-solid legal process that will eliminate any doubts when it comes to inheritance. But it can be a pain. Many states offer a simplified probate process for estates under a certain value but even a simplified process can take several months to run its course.

During this time, your heirs may not have access to their inherited assets. They have, however, acquired immediate responsibility for your funeral costs, medical and other bills, and business assets. With traditional probate, this leaves them responsible for your immediate expenses without being able to immediately access your money to pay for it. When it comes to family business assets—whether you run a restaurant, a manufacturing plant, or a family farm—any lag time can cost a family dearly.

An estate plan that includes a Living Trust allows assets to be transferred directly to heirs immediately without court proceedings. It can make an invaluable difference. However, many people are intimidated by the up-front cost of putting together an estate plan.

Probate in Illinois

Illinois has three main types of probate. The first occurs when your assets consist of personal property and are $100,000 or less. In that situation, a court proceeding may not be necessary. Instead, the lawyer can prepare a Small Estate Affidavit.

If the estate is greater than $100,000 or consists of any real estate at all, then there will most likely be a court proceeding. Once upon a time, the executor needed a court order to do any act of estate administration, which is called Supervised Administration (this is the second main type of probate in Illinois). Supervised Administration is the process in probate from which many horror stories originate. A couple of decades ago, a well-known survey found that this type of probate consumed an average 7.4 percent of an estate. As a result, states like Illinois streamlined their probate procedures.

Now Illinois has a third probate procedure called Independent Administration. This is still a court proceeding, but it is much more simplified. With Independent Administration, the executor of the estate appears in court twice: once to open the estate and then once to close the estate.

The truth is that an estate plan will cost up to $5,000 (depending on your situation). The cost of administering a trust is usually around 1 percent of the trust's value. That is 80 percent less than the potential cost of probate. What's more is that attorney fees associated with the tax planning purposes of an estate plan can be tax deductible.

When you also consider the additional tax savings that a good estate plan provides—those covered in the rest of this book—the cost of NOT having an estate plan becomes a much bigger issue than the cost of having one.

Private matters should stay private

When Michael Jackson died, the media was excitedly awaiting word about the details of his estate: How much did he have? What was it worth? Who gets what portion? We were even contacted by several reporters looking for our own speculations on the matter.

Once the court papers were filed by his attorneys and made public, the results were anticlimactic (which is actually the way we estate planning attorneys prefer such matters to end). It turns out that Michael Jackson had a decent estate plan in place—at least when it came to protecting his privacy. In the end, no juicy details of the estate were made public. Instead, to this day, the actual value of his estate remains private, locked securely inside the MICHAEL JACKSON FAMILY TRUST and away from public scrutiny.

We're not all under the microscope like Michael Jackson was, but there is value for us to keep our estate details private as well.

Certainly you've seen the infomercials or seminar invitations claiming you can "get rich quick by buying real estate." Ever wonder how they do that? It usually involves buying homes that are "probate houses." When a home is inherited through probate instead of through a trust, the details are published publicly in all their glory. That means anyone paying attention knows how much the home is really worth (not just what the owner would like to sell it for) and who it is going to. Just a little more digging can turn up information on whether or not the beneficiaries already own a home or otherwise can't afford to keep the house.

Then comes the brilliant part: deducing who most likely doesn't want or can't afford to keep the house. Those people are desperate and will either take a low bid or be forced into foreclosure. The practice of taking advantage of these vulnerable "probate houses" sounds unscrupulous, but it actually is quite legal because all of the information needed is public record.

Another reason privacy is golden: some families can be torn apart by money matters. We all have a cousin or distant relative who has always wanted what we have. He or she may be the sweetest person in the world but when money enters the picture, jealousy and greed can take over. When we're talking about people outside of our immediate families, very few legal claims can be made on the inheritance. However, when the details of who got exactly what amount of assets are public, predators will come knocking.

> *"I'm going to fight until the end. My husband is worth it."*
>
> –Anna Nicole Smith, addressing why she fought her late husband J. Howard Marshall II's son for a sizable chunk of the late oil executive's estate.

Your child may even get a call from Great Aunt Ida who has only wanted one thing in her life: a condo on Lake Tahoe. Would your child deny her that?

And don't get us started on creditors. Collection agencies will stop at nothing to collect debts. They have no problem contacting the unsuspecting relatives of debtors to make that happen—especially when they see that, from their public records searches, the unsuspecting relative just inherited a hefty sum of money. Many collection agencies will gladly prey on any relative who can foot the bill.

There are also companies that will contact heirs and pressure them to sell an inheritance for pennies on the dollar. Other companies will offer to buy an inherited annuity at a similar discount. These companies scan public court records to seek out their victims.

When it comes down to it, probate equals public record while an estate plan equals privacy. With public record, anyone can find out what you had, who inherited it, and where they live.

Which scenario would you rather create for your family?

There's no crystal ball for divorce and remarriage

Some days, we feel more like family counselors than tax advisers. We're often faced with the delicate task of pushing back the layers of emotion that can cloud good financial decisions.

If we don't teach our clients to take feelings out of the equation, they are left with financial legacies that are vulnerable to predators. We see these three common mistakes emerge over and over again when love overrules good judgment:

1. Prenuptial phobia

2. Joint tenancies "just because" (remember our initial discussion of joint tenancy in Chapter 3)

3. "I love you" wills (also called Simple Wills, discussed in Chapter 9)

Every family situation is different. But we've been in this business too long to believe that anyone's legacy is immune to the problems that come with death, divorce, and remarriage. Even if your marriage escapes the ugliness of divorce, your spouse may still opt to remarry after you die. Of course you trust his (or her) judgment when it comes to choosing a mate (he picked you, didn't he?). But being an upstanding citizen does not give your husband's new spouse the right to spend your hard-earned money.

Here's what happens all too often when prenuptial phobia, joint tenancies, and "I love you" wills take over:

1. You pass away.

2. Your spouse inherits everything.

3. Your spouse remarries.

4. Your spouse passes away.

5. New wife (or husband) inherits everything while your children inherit nothing.

What's wrong with this picture? What about your children and grandchildren? When this trifecta of poor planning is in place, your children and grandchildren suffer. Now, instead of them ultimately inheriting everything you earned, your spouse's new love walks away with it—free and clear.

Don't have your attention yet? Then let's talk about divorce.

No one thinks that they are vulnerable to divorce until it's staring them in the face. Let's say you're right: that you, and even your children, live long, happy lives in loving marriages. Now think of your grandchildren. Will you play any part in who they marry? How confident are you that even your grandchildren will marry the right people? Unfortunately in this case, statistics don't lie: divorce will strike your family at some point. And it will affect what your children and grandchildren will inherit from you.

Some states have statutes that prevent ex-spouses from accessing an inheritance under a will created during the marriage. According to the American Academy of Estate Planning Attorneys (AAEPA), some of the statutes also apply to trusts and beneficiary designations on life insurance or retirement plans. But varying state and federal laws can complicate these matters, so relying blindly on "the law" can lead to trouble.

Estate planning gives you the freedom to control as much of your legacy as you would like. In fact, you may be surprised at how much control you can have, even well after your death. An estate plan allows you to*:

- Ensure your children from a first marriage will receive the proper share of their inheritance if you remarry before you die.

- Protect assets inherited by your heirs from lawsuits, divorces, and other claims.

- Control your legacy instead of leaving it up to children or grandchildren who may not be capable or experienced in managing money.

- Ensure that a specific portion of your estate actually gets to grandchildren, charities, etc.

- Protect a portion of your estate if you pass away first and your surviving spouse remarries.

*This list was adapted from the AAEPA's Fifteen Common Reasons to Do Estate Planning, available at www.cutyourtax.com

An estate plan can also stand as an emotion-free island of authority in a sea of sensitivity and hurt feelings. Your remarrying spouse doesn't have to explain anything except, "Everything I earned with my first wife goes to my children. There's nothing I can do about it; it's just the way the trust is written."

You also don't have to insinuate that you don't trust your granddaughter's fiancé even before she marries. When she becomes a beneficiary upon your death, her response can be, "We didn't inherit a dime. All of the money is in a trust under my name but there are certain restrictions on how the money can be spent. Looks like we can't buy that Ferrari you've been wanting after all."

CHAPTER 11

How Not to Make It Work

"Talent wins games, but teamwork and intelligence wins championships."

–Michael Jordan

Why do we all hate taxes so much? It's not completely about the cost (although that certainly is a factor). It's because most of us try to do it on own either with just pen and paper or by using software like TurboTax®. And even those who enlist help will usually turn to a **CPA** for taxes, a separate investment adviser for investments, and a lawyer for wills and estate planning. These three separate professionals have their own agendas for your money and, as long as these agendas exist separately and are in competition with each other, your money will never truly work for you.

Whether you handle your finances on your own or hire too many advisers, neither scenario works because it leads to mistakes, confusion, frustration, and missed tax opportunities.

The cost of doing it yourself

Your financial legacy is different than anyone else's. The effort you put into earning and saving your money, your retirement plans, and your dreams for your family's future—these are all uniquely yours and they are continually evolving. Blindly following a cookie-cutter solution, or just doing what you've done for the past 10 years, will jeopardize these wishes and cost you dearly.

Erin Burns of *Kiplingers.com* has said, "If you own a business, own a rental property, day-trade stocks, or have other complex issues, hiring a professional could save you a lot of time and headaches."

We couldn't agree more. A huge portion of work done by tax advisers each year is to review previous years' tax returns and uncover huge discrepancies with what clients should have paid and what was actually handed over. Oftentimes this discrepancy works in favor of the IRS, meaning, many of us pay unnecessary taxes.

The government makes mistakes, too. In November 2009, controversy erupted over some mistakes that were made during the stimulus package handout to U.S. workers. It turned out that 15 million people actually owed the government some of that money back in taxes. These are mostly individuals and couples who had two sources of income and, essentially, got paid twice by the government. These very same people have somewhat complicated tax situations and should have been working with a tax adviser in the first place. By working with a tax adviser, the burden of suddenly having to pay back Uncle Sam can be mitigated using advanced tax planning techniques.

The DIY scenario is becoming more and more popular in areas outside of taxes as well. Websites like LegalZoom offer DIY legal documents for just about anything, including divorces. The problem with DIY sites like LegalZoom (which considers itself not DIY but an "automated software solution") is the false sense of security that it offers. LegalZoom's fine print will tell you that it is not a substitute for an attorney or law firm and that it only provides self-help services (not legal services) at your specific direction. Basically, you're serving as your own attorney, which means you're also solely liable.

We're not saying there isn't a place for online solutions. The Internet can be a great way to save time and money on legal preparation costs. But when your assets and tax implications surpass a certain level of complexity, only solutions that include an attorney consultation or attorney review within its process will work. When you take your chances on filling out legal documents on your own, you will never know if it was sufficient. It's your family who will ultimately discover whether or not your wishes were laid out correctly.

We often passionately argue the dangers of DIY finances with friends and family members who insist on going it alone. These people are hard-working, penny-saving teachers, policemen, and business leaders who feel that doing it on their own is a necessary responsibility that will save them money. But we ask them to look at it differently. People rely on them to do what they do best—teach, protect, provide, lead—because they are talented at what they do. Would a child learn as much sitting at home in front of a television versus being taught at school? Would a community thrive (or even survive) without a police force trained to protect and serve it? The answer is a resounding "no" to both.

People choose a profession because they are passionate about it and because they are good at it. We practice tax law because we are passionate about helping people grow, protect, and pass on their hard-earned money. Let us (the tax professionals) do that for you so that you can focus on serving others the best way you know how. In the end, the peace of mind and tax savings of using a professional will trump doing it yourself nearly every time.

The cost of having no conductor

Your money is your livelihood and your legacy, whether that money is earmarked for savings, investments, or taxes. You need a big picture planning technique to make it all work together—for you—in the right way. It's important to work with professionals.

It's even more important to enlist the help of a CPA, investment adviser, and lawyer who will work in-sync to achieve the best results. Otherwise, you will likely pay unnecessary taxes and miss out on investment opportunities because your advisers are narrowly focused on their own specialties. No one is paying attention to how it will all work together toward a common goal.

Managing your money is like conducting an orchestra. Each musician has his own part and his own technique. But it's the conductor who brings it all together to create one multi-faceted song that is balanced and beautiful (have you ever described your own financial picture as balanced and beautiful?). Perhaps during practice, the conductor will notice that the tuba is too loud or the piccolo too meager. It's the conductor who makes sure these problems are fixed so that a seamless product is produced that utilizes each musician's strengths.

Who is your conductor when it comes to your money?

The one professional usually most concerned about your final outcome is your estate planning attorney. But even estate planning attorneys can be narrowly focused on what happens at the end of your life—not on making your money work for you during your lifetime.

That's why our firm—and other firms like us—take a more holistic approach by offering tax planning, wealth management, and estate planning services all under one roof. You work with a solo professional or a small group of professionals who are mindful of making your money work together to achieve the best result. No separate agendas and no misunderstandings.

The cost of not including family in decisions

What you need to do is to train yourself to consider your entire legacy, spanning the next 50 years, instead of simply considering your year-to-year needs.

Here's a technique that has worked exceptionally well for our clients and for our own families: run your family like a business. For big decisions, gather your family into your living room. Designate someone as the CEO, another as CIO, another as a Treasurer, and so on. Decide together the pros and cons of the financial decision. How will it affect your children and grandchildren down the line? How will it affect you now? You'll be surprised at what matters and what doesn't to the rest of your family. And you'll also be able to serve as head conductor when it's time to finalize those plans with a professional.

What's more, bring your family with you as you make your estate plans and certain investment decisions. After all, aren't they the reason you're doing it in the first place? Won't they be the ones to ultimately carry out your wishes and preserve your legacy after you're gone? And shouldn't they also put together their own financial documents to help them protect their own legacies?

One of the biggest mistakes we see—especially when it comes to estate planning—is the lack of family participation in the planning process. This can have severe tax implications and can lead to any number of complications after you've passed away.

Preserving a family legacy is a team effort. Your race cannot be won when the baton is handed to a teammate who either starts running in the wrong direction or who is halted by fear and uncertainty. When this happens, Uncle Sam pulls ahead as the clear winner.

One final thought on the subject: make sure you consider your role as a benefactor and not just the one passing down the legacy. We touched on this point at the beginning of the book, but it's important enough to mention again. If you have living parents who you believe do not handle their finances appropriately, it is in your best interest to compel them to action now before it's too late. Remember that some tax laws apply to your tax bracket as the beneficiary, not theirs as the benefactors. And also keep in mind that your parents' debt and tax obligations will most likely be passed down to you as well.

Conclusion

We hope this book has given you a newfound appreciation for the art of tax planning. Filling out your tax form this April with the appropriate elections and deductions is one aspect. Putting measures in place this year that could benefit your family for decades to come is another. They are both important. And, together, these short-term and long-term strategies can save you thousands of dollars and preserve your legacy.

We invite you to look at tax planning with a purpose of empowerment. Preserve and protect what you worked hard to build. This country offers us many liberties, even when it comes to taxes. But it's your responsibility to identify and take advantage of these opportunities. Invest in what will preserve your legacy and reduce the cost of poor planning. You may never realize the true value of your accomplishments, but your family certainly will.

We wish you great fortune on your own journey and many happy [tax] returns.

Appendix

Online Resources

Illinois tax and estate planning services:
   www.cutyourtax.com (Hedeker & Perrelli)

For a professional in another state:
   www.aaepa.com or www.avvo.com

General legal information:
   www.nolo.org

Federal tax forms and information:
   www.irs.gov

Financial planning tools & advice:
   www.bankrate.com and
   www.kiplinger.com

Retirement planning tools & advice:
   www.aarp.com

Recommended Reading

The Ultimate Gift by Jim Stovall

Tax and Estate Planning Glossary of Terms

Advance Health Care Directive – Can include a Health Care Power of Attorney, Living Will, and HIPAA authorizations. These documents state what kind of treatment you would like in medical emergencies and appoint someone to make medical decisions on your behalf if you are incapacitated and unable to make your own decisions. Also referred to as an Advance Medical Directive.

Alternative Minimum Tax (AMT) – A tax that primarily affects high-income taxpayers who shelter some of their income from tax through certain tax preference items or deductions.

Asset – Any item you own that has cash or exchange value.

Beneficiary – The person(s) or organization who receives assets under a legal document such as a will, trust, or insurance policy.

Bond – A type of debt owed by federal and municipal governments and corporations. If you invest in bonds, you will usually receive interest twice a year.

C-Corp – Common business slang to distinguish a regular corporation, whose profits are taxed separate from its owners under subchapter C of the Internal Revenue Code, from an S corporation, whose profits are passed through to the shareholders and taxed on their personal income tax returns under subchapter S of the Internal Revenue Code.

Capital gain – Profit on the sale of a capital asset. Capital gains receive more favorable tax treatment than ordinary gains.

Capital loss – Loss from the sale of a capital asset. You can offset ordinary income with capital losses.

Certified Public Accountant (CPA) – A person who has met state requirements for education and work experience, passed a national exam, and met other licensing requirements. Certified public accountants (in public accounting practice) prepare tax returns, perform audits, do accounting, and give advice to their clients on financial matters.

Estate – All of the assets one owns and has an interest in at death, including real estate and investments.

Estate plan – A strategy for leaving assets to loved ones and minimizing the impact of federal and state taxes.

Estate tax – Also called the death tax. A tax imposed by the federal government and by some states on the transfer of property at death. (See related term inheritance tax.)

Executor – A person chosen by the decedent and named in the will to manage the decedent's affairs and settle the estate.

Fair market value – The price an item would sell for, assuming the buyer and seller both have reasonable knowledge and are not under undue pressure. To determine fair market value, it is common to compare other similar properties sold near the same time as your property.

Family Limited Partnership – A type of partnership comprising only related family members, usually created by parents in order to pass on a family business or investments to their children.

Fringe benefit – Employee compensation other than your wages, tips and salaries, such as health insurance, life insurance, and pension plans.

Gift tax – A graduated federal tax paid by persons who make gifts exceeding a level determined annually by the IRS.

Grantor Retained Annuity Trust (GRAT) – An estate planning technique that minimizes the tax liability existing when intergenerational transfers of estate assets occur.

HIPAA authorizations – Forms giving permission (or a waiver of permission) for the use and disclosure of your PHI/identifiable health information. These forms give your loved ones permission to use and disclose your medical information in an emergency.

Health Care Power of Attorney, also known as a Medical Power of Attorney – A power of attorney document that allows you to appoint someone to make medical decisions for you.

Health care proxy – A type of advance medical directive in which a person is named to act on someone else's behalf in a medical situation.

IRA – An Individual Retirement Account or Individual Retirement Arrangement. An IRA is a savings account for retirement. There are traditional IRAs and Roth IRAs.

Inheritance tax – An assessment on the portion of an estate received by an individual. The inheritance tax is generally determined by the amount of property received by the beneficiary, as well as by the heir's relationship to the deceased. The U.S. government levies only an estate tax. Some state governments levy inheritance and/or estate taxes.

Irrevocable trust – A trust that cannot be changed or altered. Taxable income from the trust goes to the beneficiaries or to the trust itself.

Joint tenancy – A way for two or more people to share ownership of real estate or other property. In almost all states, the co-owners (called joint tenants) must own equal shares of the property. When one joint tenant dies, the other owners automatically own the deceased owner's share.

Limited Liability Company (LLC) – A corporate structure whereby the shareholders of the company have a limited liability to the company's actions.

Living will – A legal document that allows a person to make decisions about medical treatment in advance. Living wills also include what medical treatments you would prefer and what sort of life-prolonging efforts should be made. Living wills are often created when a person has a terminal medical condition.

Money market account – A savings account that offers the competitive rate of interest (real rate) in exchange for larger-than-normal deposits.

Municipal bond – A bond issued by a state or local government. Interest you earn on a municipal bond is not subject to federal income tax.

Net worth – The amount by which assets exceed liabilities. This term can be applied to companies and individuals.

Power of Attorney – A document in which the signer authorizes someone to conduct business in his or her name. There are both Health Care Power of Attorney and Financial Power of Attorney considerations.

Probate – A state court proceeding that verifies the validity of a will or appoints an administrator to settle a decedent's estate and distribute property to heirs if there is no will. Probate may include a small estate affidavit, supervised administration, or independent administration process.

Real Estate Investment Trust (REIT) – A trust that invests primarily in real estate and mortgages and passes income, losses, and other tax items to its investors.

Revocable living trust – A trust that can be modified and altered by the grantor at any time during his or her life. The grantor can also terminate the trust during his lifetime, with all property reverting to him.

S-Corp – A corporation that meets certain requirements and elects not to be taxed as a corporation. An S-Corp does not pay federal income tax directly, but instead passes its income or losses and other tax items on to its shareholders, much like a partnership.

Section 1031 Exchange – A section of the U.S. Internal Revenue Service Code that allows investors to defer capital gains taxes on any exchange of like-kind properties for business or investment purposes.

Simple Will – Provides for the outright distribution of all assets in an uncomplicated estate and includes no itemized gifts to specific individuals.

Sole proprietorship – An unincorporated business with one owner who pays personal income tax on profits from the business.

Trust – An arrangement for holding, investing, and managing property on behalf of one or more beneficiaries.

Trustee – A person or entity named in the trust to manage the assets of a trust and distribute them according to the terms of the trust.

Will – A legal instrument used to direct the disposition of the will maker's property upon death. Also names an executor and a guardian for dependents.

Contributing sources: Bankrate.com's Estate Planning Toolkit, IRS.gov, Investopedia.com, and Nolo.

Index

401k 7, 13, 39, 45, 53
1031 Exchange 29-31, 127
2009 3-7, 24, 40-44, 49, 53, 67, 73, 110
2010 3-7, 24, 40-44, 49, 53, 67, 73, 110

A

accounting 66, 76, 121
advance and protect 3-7, 24, 40-44, 49, 53, 67, 73, 110
Advance Health Care Directive 82, 92, 120
Alternative Minimum Tax 25, 52, 120
Alzheimer's disease 89- 91
annuities 13, 40, 77
Arizona 75
assets 7, 13-15, 30, 32, 33, 36, 39, 44, 51, 52, 53, 54, 57, 59, 63, 65, 72, 76-79, 83-84, 90, 92-96, 99, 104, 111, 120, 122-123, 125, 127

B

bank account 14, 43
benefactor xi, 16, 64, 72, 76, 116
beneficiary 27, 56, 72, 76, 94, 103, 105, 116, 124
bonds 40, 43, 5-52, 54-55, 121
brokerage 13
budget 3
business 26, 28, 36, 43, 59-67, 77, 79, 85, 95, 101, 110, 112, 115, 121-122, 125, 127

buy and hold 50, 55
buy-sell agreement 62, 64

C

California 6
capital gains 7, 20, 22-25, 27-31, 49, 52, 53, 74, 127
capital loss 23, 24, 52, 53, 121
cash 3, 6, 13, 15, 51, 55, 76, 120
C-Corp 61, 62, 121
CDs 13
commodities 51
Congress 5, 66, 73-74
conversion 7, 39-41, 44-45
CPA xiii, 109, 113, 121
creditors 5, 6, 95, 100

D

deficit 3, 4, 5
depreciation 66
Disability Panel 92
Disability Trustee 92
dividends 43, 62
divorce 8, 101, 103

E

economy 6, 22, 42, 49, 50
estate documents 8
estate plan xi, 75, 78, 82-84, 89, 93, 95, 97, 98, 100, 104
estate planning 35, 71, 85, 89, 92, 97, 109, 114-115, 119, 123
Estate Tax 69, 77
estate taxes 36, 43, 71-72, 74-79, 85, 124

exemption 72, 73, 75, 77-79
exemptions 75

F
Fama-French model 50
Family Limited
 Partnership 79, 122
Family Trust 32, 84
fees 45, 66, 79, 83, 97
Financial Power of
 Attorney 92, 125
Florida 21, 30-31, 75

G
gifting 78
government loans 5
grandchildren/grandkids xi,
 xiii, 14, 16, 17, 56, 74, 76,
 102, 103, 104, 115
Grantor Retained Annuity
 Trust (GRAT) 79, 123
Gross Estate 76, 77
guardianship 90

H
HIPAA authorizations 92,
 120, 123

I
Illinois 4, 5, 6, 23, 75, 94, 96,
 119
illness 82, 90
incapacity 92
income tax 4, 5, 6, 51, 53, 58,
 59, 121, 125-127
independent
 administration 126
Indiana 76
inheritance 76, 85, 95, 99,
 100, 103-104, 122, 124
injury 82

interest 14, 43, 51-52, 63,
 116, 121-122, 125
Internal Revenue Code 121
investment v, 8, 9, 23, 28-29,
 49,-51, 53, 55, 109, 113,
 115, 127
IRA 7, 13, 38-45, 53, 56, 84,
 124
IRA Inheritance Trust 56

J
joint tenancy 26-27, 29,101-
 102, 124

L
legacy xi, xiv, 8, 16, 35, 75,
 83, 84, 101, 103-104, 109,
 113-116, 118
life insurance 13
Limited Liability Company
 (LLC) 59, 124
living trust 77-78, 93, 95
long-term investment 22, 50

M
maintenance program 8
Medicaid 93-94
medical expenses 43
mileage 65
money market account 51
mortgage 43, 79, 126
municipal bonds 51-52, 55

N
net operating loss 45, 67
net worth 14, 125

P
Pennsylvania 75
portfolio 8, 51, 55
Power of Attorney 78, 84, 92,
 120, 123, 125

prenuptial 101-102
probate 27, 77-78, 85, 93-100
property 7, 21-23, 25-31, 76, 77, 79, 93-94, 96, 110, 122, 124, 126-127

R
real estate 3, 7, 21, 42, 43, 51, 76, 96, 98, 122, 124, 126
Real Estate Investment Trust (REIT) 30-31, 126
recharacterization 40
rental property 21, 25, 30-31, 110
repairs 67
retirement 6, 7, 14, 16, 21-22, 35, 39, 41-43, 45, 83, 103, 109, 124
revenue 4, 64, 72
Revocable living trust 77, 126
risk parameters 51
Roth IRA 7, 38, 39, 40, 41, 42, 44-45, 53

S
sales tax 4, 135
savings 7, 13
savings bonds 40, 54-55
S-Corp 60-61, 126
Section 1031 Exchange 28, 127
semi-retirement 39, 42-43
S-LLC 61
Small Estate Affidavit 61
sole proprietorship 59-60, 127
spouse 16, 22, 26-28, 63, 76, 79, 83, 101-102, 104
step-up in basis 26-27, 29
stock(s) 3, 13, 39, 43, 51-52, 54, 110

stock market 3, 43, 51-52, 54, 110
Subchapter C Corporation 61
Subchapter S Corporation 61
supervised administration 126
supplies 43, 51, 52, 110
Survivor's Trust 32, 84, 126

T
tax shelter 39, 45
Texas 39, 45
travel 39, 45
trust 30, 32, 56, 77, 79, 81, 84, 93, 95, 123, 126-127
trustee 92, 127

U
unemployment 39, 45

V
vacation 39, 45
valuation 39, 45

W
wealth x-xi, xiii-xiv, 14, 36, 39, 45, 53-54, 56, 71-72, 84, 114
will 81, 82, 83, 84, 85, 92, 103, 120, 127
withdraw 53
withdrawing 15, 22, 30, 39, 44

About the Authors

Photo by Elena Bazini

Anthony R. Perrelli is a partner of Hedeker & Perrelli, Ltd. and has provided his legal expertise to the firm since 2005. He is a resident of South Barrington, Illinois (a northwestern suburb of Chicago). Anthony specializes in estate planning, estate administration, and business and tax law. He helps hundreds of families and businesses plan and preserve their legacies.

Anthony has a Bachelor's degree in accounting and an MBA with a finance concentration from Dominican University. He attended John Marshall Law School, where he earned his Juris Doctor in 2004. He is licensed to practice law in Illinois and is a member of the Chicago Bar Association, the American Bar Association, and the American Academy of Estate Planning Attorneys.

Anthony is an accomplished speaker who has led numerous estate planning seminars for individuals and businesses covering best practices in estate planning, Living Wills, and asset protection. He has been featured by *Money Magazine*, WGN News, WLS Chicago, *Bankrate.com*, and more.

Anthony welcomes your emails at aperrelli@cutyourtax.com.

Photo by Elena Bazini

Dean R. Hedeker is a leading Chicago-area authority on estate and tax planning, business law, and investments. A long-time resident of north suburban Lincolnshire, Illinois, Dean has more than 25 years' experience helping business owners and families grow, protect, and pass on their hard-earned money through tax planning, estate planning, and investment management services.

Over the past 10 years alone, Dean has created more than 2,000 estate plans and every year he handles more than 300 complex tax returns for business and families. Currently, he manages the wealth of more than 80 hard-working families.

Dean is a Certified Public Accountant (CPA) and has a Bachelor's degree and a Juris Doctor—both with highest honors—from DePaul University. He is licensed to practice law in Illinois and Pennsylvania. He is also a Registered Financial Consultant (RFC) and has served as an education adviser and Fellow of the American Academy of Estate Planning Attorneys.

Dean has made presentations at more than 500 events attended by legal, financial, and health care professionals and has been a featured source for WBBM's *Noon Business Hour*, WGN Radio, WLS Chicago, and CBS 2 Chicago. He has also co-authored three additional books: *Strictly Business: Planning Strategies for Privately Owned Businesses; Total Wealth Management; and Love, Money, Control: Reinventing Estate Planning.*

Dean welcomes your emails at dhedeker@cutyourtax.com.

Request a Free Consultation

If you are a resident of Illinois, you may be eligible for a free introductory estate planning consultation with our law firm Hedeker & Perrelli, Ltd.

Call us at (800) 201-9250, visit our website at www.cutyourtax.com, or simply mail this page to our office for more information.

Name _____

Addr _____

City/State/Zip _____

Phone _____

Email _____

Plus, sign up to receive *Cut Your Tax* updates and Hedeker & Perrelli news and information by checking your preferred delivery method: ❏ Email   ❏ Mail

Mail to: Hedeker & Perrelli
         Attn: Info Request
         One Overlook Point
         Suite 250
         Lincolnshire IL 60069

Order Copies of
Cut Your Tax in 2010

For additional copies of Cut Your Tax in 2010, please send a check to

>New Year Publishing, LLC
>144 Diablo Ranch Court
>Danville, CA 94506

$28 per copy, including sales tax

\# of copies _____

Total enclosed: $ _____

Name _____

Addr _____

City/State/Zip _____

Phone _____

Email _____

www.ingramcontent.com/pod-product-compliance
Lightning Source LLC
Chambersburg PA
CBHW070555160426
43199CB00014B/2514